# Smart Animals

# ORANGUTANS

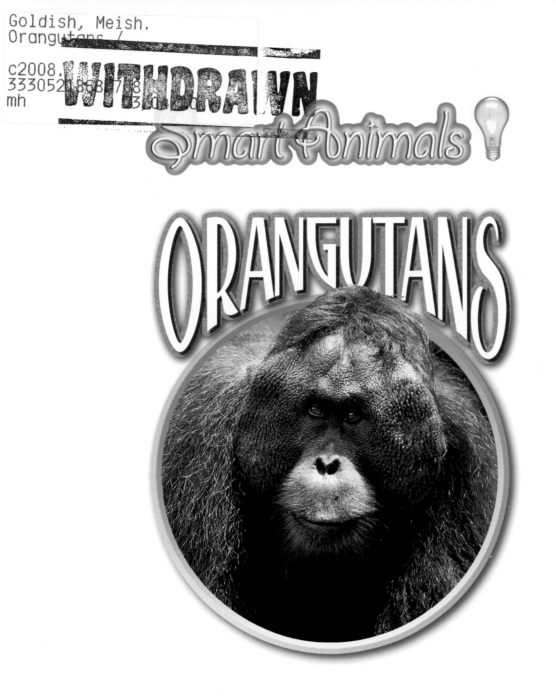

by Meish Goldish

Consultant: Gary Shapiro, Ph.D.
Cofounder/Chairman
Orang Utan Republik Education Initiative
www.orangutanrepublik.org

BEARPORT
PUBLISHING

New York, New York

**Credits**

Cover, © Frans Lanting/Minden Pictures; Title Page, © Frans Lanting/Minden Pictures; 4T, © Ralph Arbus; 4B, © Gary Shapiro, Ph.D.; 5, © Professor Anne E. Russon, Glendon College Toronto and BOS Canada; 6, © Gary Shapiro, Ph.D.; 7, © Gary Shapiro, Ph.D.; 8L, © Robert Shumaker Ph.D./Great Ape Trust of Iowa; 8R, © Robert Shumaker Ph.D /Great Ape Trust of Iowa; 9, © Smithsonian National Zoo; 11, © Rodney Brindamour/National Geographic Image Collection; 12, © Professor Anne E. Russon, Glendon College Toronto and BOS Canada; 13, © Perry van Duijnhoven; 14, © Chris Hellier/CORBIS; 15, © Mark Stouffer/Animals Animals-Earth Scenes; 16, © Perry van Duijnhoven; 17, © Rodney Brindamour/National Geographic Image Collection; 18, © Konrad Wothe/Minden Pictures; 19, © Ingo Arndt/Nature Picture Library; 20, © Anup Shah/Nature Picture Library; 21, © Andrew Murray/Nature Picture Library; 22, © Michael Nichols/National Geographic Image Collection; 23, © Shane Moore/Animals Animals-Earth Scenes; 24, © Professor Anne E. Russon, Psychology Dept., Glendon College Toronto and BOS Canada; 25, © Gerry Ellis/Minden Pictures; 26, © Nigel Dickinson/Peter Arnold; 27, © REUTERS/Bazuki Muhammad; 28, © Adam Jones/Danita Delimont/Alamy; 29T, © Stuart Conway; 29M, © Emily Sohn; 29B, © Professor Anne E.Russon, Psychology Dept., Glendon College Toronto and BOS Canada.

Publisher: Kenn Goin
Editorial Director: Adam Siegel
Creative Director: Spencer Brinker
Photo Researcher: Beaura Kathy Ringrose
Original Design: Dawn Beard Creative

*Library of Congress Cataloging-in-Publication Data*

Goldish, Meish.
 Orangutans / by Meish Goldish.
  p. cm. — (Smart animals!)
 Includes bibliographical references and index.
 ISBN-13: 978-1-59716-578-5 (library binding)
 ISBN-10: 1-59716-578-6 (library binding)
 1. Orangutan—Juvenile literature. I. Title.

QL737.P96G566 2008
599.88'3—dc22

2007030332

For more information, write to Bearport Publishing Company, Inc., 101 Fifth Avenue, Suite 6R, New York, New York 10003. Printed in the United States of America.

10 9 8 7 6 5 4 3 2 1

# Contents

# A Clever Princess

Princess had a problem. She wanted some food that was locked in a **storeroom**. Yet Princess didn't have a key. What could she do to get the food?

▲ **Princess is an orangutan that was born on the island of Borneo in Southeast Asia.**

▲ **Princess as a baby**

First, Princess picked up a stick. Next, she bit the end until it fit inside the keyhole. She poked the "stick key" through the hole and wiggled it back and forth. At last the lock opened.

Princess didn't need someone else's key to solve her problem. She was smart enough to make her own!

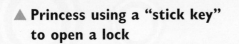

▲ **Princess using a "stick key" to open a lock**

Orangutans belong to a group of animals called great apes. Chimpanzees, **bonobos**, and gorillas are also smart animals in this group.

# Signs of Language

Scientists studied Princess to see how intelligent she was. They wondered if she could learn to **communicate** with people by using **American Sign Language**. Other scientists had taught chimpanzees and gorillas how to make the hand movements that stand for different words. Could orangutans learn this language, too?

▲ **Dr. Gary Shapiro teaching sign language to Princesss**

Dr. Gary Shapiro taught Princess for two years. She was a good student. Between 1978 and 1980, she learned more than 30 **signs**. Princess used them to name objects and express her needs. She used some signs when she wanted food. She used other signs when she wanted to be tickled or to have her hair combed. She even combined signs to describe new things. After tasting pineapple for the first time she signed "sweet fruit."

Princess was able to use sign language to make simple sentences, such as "You there scratch."

▲ **Princess and Dr. Gary Shapiro take a swim together.**

# Using a Computer

Princess used sign language to communicate. Dr. Robert Shumaker taught Azy (AY-zee) and his sister, Indah (IN-duh), to communicate using **symbols** on a computer screen. Each symbol stood for a different word, such as *grapes*, *cup*, *carrot*, or *ball*.

▲ **Azy**　　　　　　　　　　　　　　　　▲ **Indah**

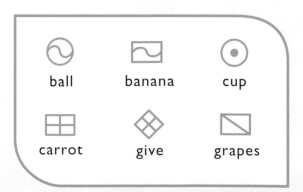

| | | |
|---|---|---|
| ⊘ ball | ∿ banana | ⊙ cup |
| ⊞ carrot | ◈ give | ◹ grapes |

▲ These are some of the symbols Azy and Indah learned.

Azy and Indah learned symbols that do not look like the things they stand for.

8

After learning the symbols, Azy was shown some grapes. A few different symbols then appeared on his computer screen. Azy looked at them and then touched the symbol for grapes. As a reward, he got to eat the sweet fruit.

Indah made simple sentences with the symbols she learned. One day she saw a closed cup filled with food. She then touched the symbols for *open* and *cup*. It was clear what she wanted!

◀ **Azy touching the symbol for grapes**

# Learning in the Wild

Azy and Indah were taught many of their **skills** at the National Zoo in Washington, D.C. Yet most orangutans live in the wild. How smart are they? A scientist named Dr. Biruté Galdikas found the answer. In 1971, she traveled to a **rain forest** on the island of Borneo and set up Camp Leakey. There, she and other scientists studied wild orangutans for more than 30 years.

## Orangutans in the Wild

Where orangutans live

▲ **Borneo and Sumatra are islands in Southeast Asia. They are the only two places in the world where wild orangutans live.**

Dr. Galdikas learned a lot by watching orangutans in their natural **habitat**. She found that a baby orangutan stays close to its mother for several years. The mother teaches her baby how to survive. For example, each night orangutans build nests in trees for sleeping. Young orangutans learn how to make nests by watching their mothers build them.

Young orangutans learn from their mothers which foods are good to eat. They also learn how to test which tree branches are strong enough to hold them.

◀ **Biruté Galdikas at Camp Leakey**

## Sounding Off

At Camp Leakey, Dr. Galdikas learned about a sound that adult males make to communicate. It is a roar that can be heard up to about one mile (1.6 km) away. This "long call" invites female orangutans to join a male so that they can **mate**. It also warns other males to stay away.

The long call of a male orangutan can last up to two minutes.

Besides the long call, orangutans make other sounds to communicate. If an enemy is near, an orangutan may make a "kiss-squeak" sound. The kiss-squeak lets the enemy know it has been discovered. The **predator** may then leave the area, as it can no longer catch the orangutan by surprise.

▲ **This orangutan is making a kiss-squeak sound.**

# Making Tools

Making and using **tools** is a sign of a smart animal. For many years, scientists thought that chimpanzees were the only apes in the wild that used tools. In the 1990s, however, scientists made a surprising discovery. They saw orangutans using sticks as tools to get food.

Orangutans shape their tools by biting and chewing them. They may bite off part of a stick to shorten it or chew on a stick's end to give it a sharper point.

Sometimes the orangutans pushed sticks into bee nests. When they pulled the sticks out, they were covered with honey. The orangutans could now eat the honey-covered sticks like lollipops. Other times the clever orange apes poked sticks into **termite** nests. They flicked out the tasty insects and ate them.

▲ This orangutan pokes a stick into a termite nest to get the insects inside.

# Tools for Food

Orangutans use sticks to get more than just honey and insects. The fruit of the *Neesia* tree has tasty seeds inside. Orangutans love to eat them. However, the inside of the fruit is filled with sharp, stinging hairs. It is very painful if the orangutan touches them. How do the clever apes safely get the seeds out? They use a thin stick as a tool.

▲ **Orangutans use a stick to get seeds out of the *Neesia* fruit.**

Orangutans are good at remembering where different kinds of fruit trees grow in the rain forest. They also know when the fruit on each tree is ripe.

First, an orangutan slides a stick into a crack in the fruit. By moving the stick around, the seeds become loose. The orangutan can now shake out the seeds and eat them without getting stuck by the prickly hairs inside.

▲ **This orangutan uses a stick to open a coconut.**

# Group Learning

Not all orangutans use tools. Dr. Carel van Schaik studied different groups of orangutans in the wild. He found that only some of them make and use tools. How did those orangutans learn their skills?

In Sumatra, orangutans on one side of a river know how to use sticks to get seeds out of a fruit. Orangutans on the other side of the same river, however, do not.

In some groups, older orangutans had figured out how to use tools. Younger orangutans in the group closely watched the "teachers." Then they copied the actions. After about seven years of practice, the young orangutans became good at making and using tools, too.

In other places where orangutans live, the animals do not use tools. The orangutans have not discovered the skill, so it cannot be taught to others.

▲ **This orangutan eats a nest of termites without using any tools.**

# Acting Human

Orangutans in the wild do many things that make them seem almost human. They use leaves as napkins. They swat flies with leafy branches. They use sticks to scratch themselves. They are even able to keep out the sun or rain by building a nest with a roof of leaves. Orangutans learn these skills by watching other orangutans in the wild.

The word *orangutan* means "person of the forest" in the Malay language, which is spoken by people in Southeast Asia.

▲ **Orangutans in the wild use leaves to protect themselves from the sun.**

Orangutans in **captivity** learn skills in another way. They watch how humans behave. Then they copy the actions. These orangutans can wash laundry, hammer nails, saw wood, and use a screwdriver. They are able to take a canoe for a boat ride. They can even eat food using plates and spoons.

◀ **Princess learned how to wash clothes by watching people do it.**

# Brain Champs

It is clear that orangutans are smart. Yet how do they compare with other intelligent animals? In a recent study, scientists tested 25 different nonhuman **primates**. They were judged on how well they could solve problems and learn. Orangutans were found to be the smartest.

▲ **Like orangutans, chimpanzees are smart animals that make and use tools. This chimpanzee uses a twig to get ants out of a tree.**

For years, many people thought that chimpanzees were the smartest of all nonhuman primates. Now some scientists have put orangutans at the top of the list. What makes these apes so smart? Some scientists think it is because orangutans spend so much time in trees. They have no enemies up there. As a result, their brains have more time to grow and develop.

Wild female orangutans spend 99 percent of the time in trees.

## Special Feelings

Unyuk is an orangutan smart enough to fool people. One day she was playing with a scientist. He pretended to be cutting the ape's hair. As Unyuk played along, she edged closer to his side. Suddenly, she made her move. Unyuk tried to grab the scientist's backpack. She had been planning to snatch the bag all along!

▲ **Unyuk with her son Udik**

Orangutans are able to pretend that they are not paying attention when in fact they really are watching something.

Orangutans like Unyuk have **emotional** intelligence. They show different moods in the way they behave. Sometimes orangutans will act playful, gentle, and loving. Other times they may be angry or jealous.

▲ **These young orangutans are playing together.**

# Protecting Orangutans

Orangutans are smart enough to use tools, solve problems, and communicate with people. Yet they are still struggling to survive.

Some families in Asia want baby pet orangutans. To get them, **poachers** must kill the mothers. Many orangutans are murdered each year.

Orangutans also suffer because their homes are destroyed. Trees in the rain forests are cut down so that the wood can be sold. The trees are also set on fire to clear the land for farming.

▲ **In the last 20 years, 80 percent of the orangutan's habitat has been destroyed.**

Fortunately, people have found ways to help orangutans. They raise the babies whose mothers were killed. They teach them skills to live in the wild. Other people work to protect the rain forests. With their help, there is hope that these clever orange apes will continue to survive.

Orangutans are an **endangered species**. Since 1990, the wild orangutan **population** has been reduced by about 50 percent.

▲ **These orangutans are being taken care of at a rescue center.**

# Just the Facts

## Orangutan

| | |
|---|---|
| **Weight** | males: 170–300 pounds (77–136 kg) <br> females: 66–110 pounds (30–50 kg) |
| **Height** | males: 3.2–4.5 feet (1–1.4 m) <br> females: 2.6–3.5 feet (.8–1 m) |
| **Food** | fruit, leaves, bark, flowers, shoots, bird eggs, ants, larvae, and termites |
| **Life Span** | about 40–50 years in the wild; <br> about 50–60 years in captivity |
| **Habitat** | the rain forests of Borneo and northern Sumatra |
| **Population** | 50,000–60,000 in the wild (about 6,700 in Sumatra; the rest are in Borneo) |

## More Smart Orangutans

An orangutan named Chantek lives at Zoo Atlanta in Georgia. He knows more than 150 words in American Sign Language. Born in captivity, Chantek has learned many skills over the years. He is able to clean his room. He can help cook spaghetti. Chantek is even good at making jewelry. He places beads on a string to make necklaces.

▲ **Chantek**

**A necklace made** ▶
**by Chantek**

Supinah is an orangutan at Camp Leakey in Borneo. She has learned many skills by watching humans. She can hammer nails and saw wood. The clever ape can paint buildings and sweep porches. She even knows how to make pancake batter by mixing eggs and flour. Supinah uses a cup and a spoon as tools to help her.

◀ **Supinah sawing**
**wood**

# Glossary

**American Sign Language** (uh-MER-uh-kuhn SINE LANG-gwij) a language that is used instead of spoken words; it is made up of hand and body movements, as well as facial expressions, and is often used by people who can't hear

**bonobos** (buh-NOH-bohz) a kind of great ape, also known as pygmy chimpanzees, that live in Central Africa

**captivity** (kap-TIV-uh-tee) being held in a place that is not one's natural home and from which one cannot leave

**communicate** (kuh-MYOO-nuh-kate) to share information, wants, needs, and feelings

**emotional** (i-MOH-shuh-nuhl) having to do with one's feelings

**endangered species** (en-DAYN-jurd SPEE-sheez) a kind of animal that is in danger of dying out; no more will be left on Earth

**habitat** (HAB-uh-*tat*) a place in nature where a plant or animal normally lives

**mate** (MATE) to come together to have young

**poachers** (POHCH-urz) people who hunt illegally

**population** (*pop*-yuh-LAY-shuhn) the total number of a kind of animal living in a place

**predator** (PRED-uh-tur) an animal that hunts other animals for food

**primates** (PRYE-mates) members of the group of smart animals that includes humans, monkeys, and apes

**rain forest** (RAYN FOR-ist) a warm place where many trees grow and lots of rain falls

**signs** (SYNEZ) hand movements that stand for words

**skills** (SKILZ) the abilities to do things well

**storeroom** (STOR-room) a room where food, equipment, or supplies are kept

**symbols** (SIM-buhlz) things that stand for or represent other things

**termite** (TUR-mite) an insect that is like an ant and eats wood

**tools** (TOOLZ) objects that are used to do a job

30

# Bibliography

**Gallardo, Evelyn.** *Among the Orangutans: The Biruté Galdikas Story.* San Francisco: Chronicle Books (1993).

**Lindsey, Jennifer.** *The Great Apes.* New York: MetroBooks (1999).

**Russon, Anne E.** *Orangutans: Wizards of the Rainforest.* Buffalo, NY: Firefly Books (2004).

**Shumaker, Robert W.** *Orangutans.* St. Paul, MN: Voyageur Press (2007).

**Shumaker, Robert W., and Benjamin B. Beck.** *Primates in Question.* Washington, D.C.: Smithsonian Books (2003).

**van Schaik, Carel.** *Among Orangutans: Red Apes and the Rise of Human Culture.* Cambridge, MA: Belknap Press of Harvard University Press (2004).

**www.orangutanrepublik.org** (Orang Utan Republik Education Initiative)

# Read More

**Darling, Kathy, and Tara Darling.** *How to Babysit an Orangutan.* New York: Walker and Company (1996).

**Dixon, Dougal.** *Orangutan Rescue.* Columbus, OH: Waterbird Books (2004).

**Martin, Patricia A. Fink.** *Orangutans.* Danbury, CT: Children's Press (2000).

**Orme, Helen.** *Orangutans in Danger (Wildlife Survival).* New York: Bearport Publishing (2007).

**Steele, Christy.** *Orangutans.* Austin, TX: Raintree Steck-Vaughn (2001).

# Learn More Online

To learn more about orangutans, visit
**www.bearportpublishing.com/SmartAnimals**

# Index

## About the Author

Meish Goldish has written more than 100 books for children. He lives in Brooklyn, New York.